Of gossamers and grace

poems by

Bill Denham

Finishing Line Press
Georgetown, Kentucky

Of gossamers and grace

Editor: Christen Kincaid

Author Photo: Linda Elvira Piedra

Cover Design: Elizabeth Maines

Printed in the USA on acid-free paper.
Order online: www.finishinglinepress.com
              also available on amazon.com

Author inquiries and mail orders:
Finishing Line Press
P. O. Box 1626
Georgetown, Kentucky 40324
U. S. A.

Table of Contents

This book is dedicated to June Todd Smith

Foreword

From the pen of a young woman, a senior at James A. Gray High School in Winston-Salem, North Carolina, in the year 1959, came these words, on an evening when she was babysitting the children of a neighborhood family.

> I prayed to see my Bill tonight,
> But God seemed not to think
> That he and I'd be coupled right—
> That our thoughts would not link.
>
> I pray that God would give to me
> An evening with my Bill,
> Moments of joy and love and glee,
> To flood my heart with thrill.
>
> I pray my Bill would of me know,
> The way I of him dream;
> And that his thoughts would ever grow
> Of us, as love in team.
>
> Although this love may foolish be
> As schoolgirl crushes will,
> I pray one day our God may see
> As one, me and my Bill.

I had no knowledge of these words until she recited them by heart, more than fifty years later when we both found ourselves at our 50th high school reunion, meeting for the first time in half a century. June Quackenbush and I had been friends in high school but not at all romantically involved.

What follows, then, is a bit of a surprising love story—a baker's dozen moments captured in verse on what has now become our remarkable, joint journey.

Bill Denham
Portland, Oregon
November 10, 2014

One

I had forgotten the sourwood flowers

I had forgotten the sourwood flowers
>in late summer seen
>scattered across the valley floor
>and halfway up the mountainside
>but not the sounds of water tumbling,
>falling over and around and among
>those ancient stones,
>nor that particular, peculiar way she shrugged
>and tilted her head to both acknowledge
>and to deflect a moment of connection.

I had forgotten much,
>yet, this gesture, remembered, fifty years out—
>did touch somewhere near the source
>that flows from underneath
>the surface.

November 5, 2009

Two

Love poem

You do not make me who I am
> any more than I make you who you are
> but there is a miracle that happens inside of me
> when I know and feel your love,
> that I can only liken to a moment of conception,
> that split second when a whole new being begins—
> two become one and divide and divide and divide
> and take shape around a mystery, yet to be known.

January 7, 2010

Three

Peas in a pod

Listen, I am thinking, now,
       of the two old people,
       so young at heart
       that they might, at any moment,
       catch the other's eye
       and break open with smiles and giggles
       at the pure joy of being old
       and having found each other.

"Peas in a pod," he says,
       from time to time,
       at a delightfully unexpected convergence
       of feeling, of idea or experience shared—
       the end of loneliness
       and an unstoppable upwelling,
       like spring water rising
       through the fissures and the cracks,
       this gratitude welling up
       and breaking through the years
       that have been laid down upon the years—
       Thank you their mantra—
       words spoken by each to each,
       spoken to everyone
       and spoken to no one in particular,
       forever fresh and always young—
       these two words, *thank you.*

April 15, 2010

Four

Point Reyes—wild oats in the wind

As if it were the holy spirit
       engulfing me,
       as if I even knew
       the nature of such a thing,
       as if I might even be able to tell you
       the mystery of a moment that pushed me
       to the very edge of . . . of . . . something,
       calling loudly, without words,
for me to simply open up—all the way . . .

We stood together in silence,
       in the midst of things,
       on the headlands, high above the surf,
       a dusty trail beneath our feet
       crisscrossed from time to time
       by slow moving, shiny black beetles,
       while stationary, high above our heads
       a hawk lay just beneath the cold gray blanket
       that covered everything on this tiny slip of land
       sliding northward, sliding always northward.
       And everywhere it was wind—
       the air moved, ruffled clothes and tousled hair,
       made soft staccato pops and flutters in our ears
       that almost hid from them
       an exquisite, near silent song.

Had we not seen the wild oats dancing,
        delicately dangling their tiny, hull-covered seeds,
        atop straight golden stalks,
        that bent down in the wind,
        as if to say, *namaste*, to everything,
        lightly touching one another, then,
        like bows and strings—
        had we not seen them dancing so,
        we would have missed their music,
        their heavenly music,
        the intricacy of which,
        the joy of which
        went well beyond
        what human hand
        could make
        or these human words
        describe.

Oh, the wind and the song of the wild oats!

July 9, 2010

Five

Space—
through the eye of the Hubble

I

I caught her eye—
      for a split second—
      deep and black as space,
      as she caught mine
      and spoke the words, "Thank you."
      And in that instant, in that blackness, I saw the universe,
      as if my eye were Hubble itself,
      looking deep to the very edge of things,
      as if I had no choice but see her sorrow,
      her beauty, as she saw mine—
      in an instant.

II

It was imperfect, at first,
      the Hubble and one might argue, still,
      as the images it receives and passes on
      bend and stretch our psyches
      as if we too were made of light,
      push us into that cloud of unknowing
      where words fall weightless
      and awe is all
      there is—
      and mystery.
      And so we feel
      the beginning,
      we feel
      our heart
      break open.

III

It was the most mundane of encounters.
I had held the door for the wheelchair bound
elderly man I took to be her husband—
nothing strange, what anyone might do.
But the moment was not ordinary.
We were coming, all of us, from the same place.
And though we were strangers
and likely to never see one another again,
we had shared an hour
that left us, at once,
profoundly different
and exactly the same.
We had born witness
to the birth of stars—
star nurseries they were called,
giant nebula given ancient names like Carina,
the ship keel constellation of the southern sky
within which mountains and canyons
of frozen gas and dust might rise or fall
near twenty trillion miles—
one called *Mystic Mountain*
whose double spires
are topped by infant stars
flinging their signature streamers of gas
untold distances into the heavens . . .

oh, my . . . oh, my . . . how even this attempt
to restore a speck of weight to our words falls short
and we are left, as if our hearts were supernovae
blown wide open and brilliant
before fading toward death.

IV

And so it was as we left the theater,
  my dear companion weeping
  and I nearly so,
  stood in the corridor
  unable to move
  toward the stairs
  when a group
  approached,
  led by the
  fallen patriarch,
  pushed in his wheelchair
  by one I thought to be his daughter,
  flanked and followed by several others
  and finally the wife and mother
  whose small stature belied
  the universe I found
  in her eyes.

August 24, 2010

Six

The other

I had opened the door,
        partially, on the driver side,
        of my low-hung, long, red,
        classic, eighty-five Volvo wagon.
        Grimacing with pain, I carefully,
        slowly turned my body to the left,
        took my hand from the door,
        lifted my left leg up and over
        and dropped it to the ground.

When looking up I saw his face
        framed by the shiny black metal door
        of the huge Tundra, towering over me
        rolling slowly past on its gigantic tires
        and framed as well by his shiny black hair,
        pulled back smooth and tight—
        this strikingly beautiful young brown face
        with black indigenous eyes
        looking out and down upon me—
        old, poor and white,
        this young brown man
        had rolled his window down,
        never mind it simply meant pushing a button,
        he opened his window to ask,
        as I struggled to get out
        and to straighten my knee,
        "Are you, OK? Need help?"
        "No," I hollered, with a smile,
        "Just gotta straighten
        this fuckin' knee o' mine. Thanks, anyway."

He went on. I went on,
        walked around a bit,
        got back in the car,
        pulled into the slow moving traffic
        behind a big eighteen wheeler
        and headed over the Richmond-San Rafael bridge
                toward home.
        We had wanted to make it home without stopping
        but my knee had other ideas—
        like somebody was driving a spike
        right down the middle of it
        and coming out the left side.

Next morning, I woke early, in the dark
        and saw his face—
        this young brown face, riding high
        in his buddy's black Tundra,
        looking down on me. And I saw him.
        Looking up, I saw him, felt him
        and my sweet love held me, in the dark,
        as I told her what I saw
        and wept.

November 5, 2010

Seven

A love story

Now, you may not believe this
>   but if the wisdom of age
>   and experience counts for anything,
>   let me tell you, I have just begun
>   my seventieth year on this earth.

When I gazed into her face
>   framed by the beige and brown
>   of the pillows and the auburn gray curl of her hair,
>   the freckles I had known all those years ago, were there
>   but it was the shape, the tone and the expression,
>   the unforgettable expression of openness,
>   warm and as natural as the morning sun's rays
>   that fell across our bed, as we were saying good bye
>   and *Thank you*, the way we always do.

You must understand this miracle,
>   for my sweet love has Parkinson's
>   and Parkinson's has a way with faces
>   and with bodies and movement—
>   has a way with expression.

But what came through to me
        on this last morning of our visit
        as we held each other
        was pure soul, that same
        pure soul I had known
        in some peripheral way
        a half a century ago
        in the high school hallways
        and classrooms we had shared

And now, in the mysterious way of things,
        having been fifty years apart
        we have come together—
        I, no longer ignorant of myself
        nor of her high school prayer
        that we might one day be one.
        Hardly any wonder, then,
        our mantra,
        Thank you.

November 10, 2010

Eight

Winter solstice

On our way to bed
        we found ourselves
        on opposite corners
        of the old four poster,
        at the foot,
        she on the right, me on the left,
        she doing the Parkinson's shuffle
        me doing the spinal-tumor bend[1]
        and catching each others eye
        the way we do, we began to giggle
        and our giggles swelled to belly laughs
        that were so painful to my pinched nerves
        that I nearly fell on the floor from mirth and pain
        all wrapped up in a glorious moment, in perfect harmony
        with the glories of the season, the darkest night
                of the year.

But lest you think we are entirely crazy,
        let me share a saner moment:
        at 4:00AM or maybe 3:30,
        we each awoke with a need to potty—
        Parkinson's meds and enlarged prostates
        result in this kind of moment, day or night.
        As we sleepily met back in bed, my love asked me:
        "How would you categorize these poets?"
        She referred to the book we'd been reading
                each evening before bedtime:
        Fooling with Words by Bill Moyers, a compilation of
                interviews

with a number of poets at the Geraldine R Dodge Poetry
        Festival in '98
In my sleepy stupor, I stumbled around a bit and said not
        much of anything
while my love, still engaged, offered this observation:
"They all are responding to the needs of the culture"—
by which she meant, if not already obvious, that these
        are poets of the soul
who are beacons for us in the darkness of this world.
By then I was wide awake and full of gratitude
for my good fortune . . . it was some time
before the warmth of our bodies together
lulled me back to sleep.

---

[1] On December 9, 2010, following an MRI of my lower back, I was diagnosed
with a small benign tumor growing within my spinal cord dura between L2 and
L3. The tumor accompanied me on my Christmas visit to see June and was
subsequently surgically removed on February 17, 2011.

December 23, 2010

Nine

Namaste

In silence
        and in the darkness
        she drew me to herself
        and held me
        in a strong and steady way,
        no twitch nor tremor,
        not a hint of Parkinson's.
        I cannot tell you
        how long we lay so,
        motionless,
        save for the slow and rhythmic breath
        that came and went from our two bodies
        nor how long it was before
        I gave sound to my gratitude,
        whispered softly, *thank you*,
        nor how long before she spoke
        those few words
        in so clear and simple a way
        I knew myself to be divine
        and in the presence of divinity,
        such is the power
        of honest words
        spoken from an open
        trustful heart
        to another.

I can tell you this much.
　　　　I need tell you no more—
　　　　not what passed before
　　　　nor what came after—
　　　　for you to know the nature
　　　　of this intricate
　　　　dance we dance,
　　　　called *life* or *love*
　　　　or both.

January 2, 2011

Ten

Of gossamers and grace

I

In naughts and ones
        our words fly out
        into the ether, each evening,
        land six hundred miles away
        upon our ears
        as spoken sound,
        in the way of magic—
        not unlike that of old
        when all were one with all,
        and words themselves could make of us,
        this or that, simply by the speaking
        or even by the thought.

And when I speak to you so—unseen—
        the patterns, the pauses,
        the rhythms and intonations,
        the slightly Southern echoes of my speech
        call up in you—gossamer-like reveries,
        faint memories of my manner
        a half century gone,
        that are there, in me still—
        you see the youth,
        engagingly earnest,
        leaning, perhaps,
        slightly forward,
        a tilt to his head,
        at the left front corner
        of the teacher's large oak desk

and then suddenly, unexpectedly
from out of your reverie,
you sometimes speak my name
in a soft questioning way
that holds both disbelief and affirmation, too—
knowing somehow in the depths of yourself
that I am one with that young man.

And what this means to me is more than I can tell
but I shall try, my dear, I shall try . . .

II

As one fallen
knows desolation and the pit,
knows even more the weight born,
when by dint of will alone
and help from others
he claws his way up and out,
sees more clearly, at each new step
the harm done to self and those he thought to love—
so, too, he knows the echoes, echoes of doubt,
growing fainter, hardly audible
yet there, always there,
near silent whisperings come . . .

Who . . . ? Who am I . . . ?
Who was I before the fall?

for which there is no answer
inside himself, no way of knowing,
no way back.

III

Yet as August sunlight breaks
        above the gabled house,
        over the eastern hills,
        catching unseen gossamer strands
        that fall from branch or leaf,
        float down, in iridescence,
        and find, then, an anchor,
        a starting point,
        so these faint, recurring memories of me—a youth,
        strong with resemblance to now,
        break across my soul, each time
        you speak my name so quietly,
        with wonder, with curiosity and a certain joy
        and find that anchor point in my heart,
        and give that gift of life, that place to start
        and quiet the whispering echoes of my doubts.

And so you held me in your heart these many years
        and give back, now, these spoken memories—
        with not a single forethought,
        a pure and simple gift of grace,
        of saving grace—like the magic,
        of old—that makes us One.

June 1, 2011

Eleven

My shining one

There is a way I have
of loving you
that seems to set you free.
I can't explain it.
I see and feel it,
as if the years melt away
and that spirit that has been there
from the beginning
brings the pure beauty
from inside out
and the pathways
in your brain,
laid down
those decades ago
are somehow remembered
and the multitude of muscles
in your face, 'round your eyes,
'round your mouth, from forehead to cheek to chin
relax and speak an innocent purity
as if your face were the soft flame of love, itself,
the very essence of shining
and when you move, then,
those same pathways re-discovered, opened up again,
gift your body a buoyancy and grace,
a boogie and a flow,
that brings me
to my knees
in gratitude
to see you so,
oh, my shining one.

July 14, 2011

Twelve

Amazement

Expectant, as one,
    we waited on the canyon rim
    our backs to the limber pine.
    The sinking sun's bending rays
    threw long hoodoo shadows
    across their neighbors' tortured shapes,
    those ranks—both red and white—
    of fellow limestone fins and columns,
    while far across the distant valley,
    on the Eastern horizon,
    resting gently atop the verdant slope
    just below the peak,
    like a giant knitted cap,
    three softly rounded clouds,
    were being painted by these very rays,
    a delicate, ever darkening, pink patina
    and just above the peak
    and slightly to the right,
    the pale, mottled face
    of a white, full moon
    climbed slowly higher,
    shrinking, as it grew more bright,
    casting magic over all.

And when those fleeting rays
    ricocheted off the hoodoo crowns—
    the thin, hard, gray layers atop each column,
    laid down some thirty million years ago or more
    when Bryce Canyon was no canyon at all
    but a simple low place on the earth,

where rain and floods brought sediments
from the mountains, all around, and left them there—
they shone like a chain of crystal lakes
scattered before towering red cliffs.
At least, one could imagine them so,
as my sweet love had done,
before putting words to her imaginings,
and sharing, quietly whispering,
"They look like water."

And so they did and so I knew, yet,
        another layer of amazement.

September 26, 2013

Thirteen

Frozen

My love is no Snow Queen,
  though we do speak,
  with some regularity,
  the word frozen
  or the words freezing up
  to describe her state—
  an apt metaphor
  when I see her feet
  unable to move
  as if they were frozen in place,
  frozen to the carpet,
  a book in hand,
  frozen to the tarmac,
  waiting, the car door open,
  frozen to the lawn,
  in her particular Parkinson's limbo,
  shears and trimmings
  held out for balance,
  as if making an offering,
  or a supplication.

But this disease of diminishment
　　　　does not touch her heart,
　　　　her large, warm, playful,
　　　　open heart that moves
　　　　with ease from tango
　　　　to waltz to jitterbug,
　　　　from minuet to bebop,
　　　　and so we take what is
　　　　and laugh and weep
　　　　and dance our way
　　　　through each day.

Epilogue

A pause on this day to simply say . . .

There is more that I could tell
        but the darkness that was around me
        in the early morning hours
        as I lay awake, is no more.
        It is gone.
        It always wanes.
        And though I know
        its necessity
        and know its function
        and know its beauty
        and know the grace, even, of darkness,
        I am grateful, yet again,
        for the coming of the light
        and the slow arrival of color,
        for the changing shapes,
        for the hidden things made known,
        for this warmth splashing
        across my life.

Bill Denham

On December 27, 2013,
June and I
were married
at the
Multnomah County Administration Building
in
Portland, Oregon

Acknowledgments

These poems grew out of my relationship with the person I know
as June Quakenbush. Without June there would be no poems.
And without our mutual friend and high school classmate,
June Todd (Smith) who invited each of us separately
to attend our 50th high school reunion,
there would be no poems.
But without the
suggestion from my friend, Liz Weiner,
that I submit my manuscript to the Finishing
Line Press, this little chapbook would not exist and,
of course, without all the love and support of my family
and friends over the years, I would never have arrived at the
place of being able to share myself in this way.
Finally, without you, the reader or speaker,
this little chapbook would have
no meaning. So, thanks, to all.

Educated in the South at Davidson College and at UC Berkeley in the mid-sixties where he received his MA in English Literature, Bill Denham rejected a promising academic career after five years of teaching at Luther College and the University of Hawaii to go back to the land in the mountains of West Virginia. His subsequent journey of self discovery has been turbulent, painful but ultimately rewarding.

Now, in his mid-70s, he is a retired letterpress printer from Painted Tongue Press in Oakland, California, where his collection of intricate paper sculptures still hang from the ceiling. He relocated to Portland, Oregon, in 2013, to be with an old high school classmate, June Quackenbush, after they reconnected at their 50th high school reunion in '09 in Winston-Salem, NC.

He published a single volume of poetry in 2013, *Looking for Matthew*— seventeen lyric and narrative poems that explore his own grief and responsibility following the street slaying of Matthew Avery Solomon on September 4, 2008. His poem, Do you remember, Dad?, appeared in the anthology, *Daring to Repair* (Wising Up Press, 2012). Other poems have been shared widely among friends and colleagues at poetry salons and spoken word events and have appeared online over the years, primarily in his postings, *More morning musings from the land of the open heart*, through the listserv for The Redwood Men's Center (redwoodmen.org).

CPSIA information can be obtained
at www.ICGtesting.com
Printed in the USA
LVHW080915291221
707409LV00020B/560